Words He Will Never Read

Kathryn Rowlands

BookLeaf Publishing

India | USA | UK

Presentation by *BookLeaf Publishing*

Web: www.bookleafpub.com

E-mail: info@bookleafpub.com

ISBN: 9789394788503

First edition 2022

DEDICATION

In memory of Alexander Parsons

ACKNOWLEDGEMENT

To Alexander - I will take a lifetime of overflowing grief to have held you in my arms for eight and a half months. I will forever be the proudest Mother to the most wonderful son.

To Jon - thank you for continuing beside me through this journey, for picking me up off the floor when my legs couldn't continue, and for being the best Father our beautiful boy could have wanted. We were a part of him, and you will always be a part of me.

To all of my family and friends - your love, support and kind words have meant more than I have been able to express. I am not the person I was before, but I love and thank you all endlessly.

Overflowing

Unspent love,
overflows
into grief,
overflows
into words
on a page.

Red

I thought Blue would be the colour surrounding my memories of
you. From your piercing eyes that filled me with pride, to the frozen
Icelandic waterfall we visited on what happened to be our only
family holiday. But all I can see is Red.
Red. The colour of the rash that danced across your skin – first on
your chest and back, and then swirling down your arms and legs.
Red. The colour of your eyes for the weeks leading to your death.
Thunderbolts of crimson scattering the white that surrounded your
navy-lined irises.
Red. The colour of your strawberry-tainted lips – unnaturally so
because every blood vessel in your body was inflamed – fighting
an illness no longer causing your body harm. An overreaction of
your immune system that for some reason cannot be controlled.

Red. The colour of the palms of your hands and the soles of your
feet – distinctively classic for Kawasaki Disease. Like a neon arrow
flashing as a warning sign for an illness that would be caught 'early
enough' to not warrant thinking about the possibility that your story
might end the way it did.
Red. The colour of danger. Of anger. Of love. Of hearts. How I can't
escape every time my fingers grasp a pen to draw a simple heart
and an electric shock temporarily disables me. We don't like hearts
anymore. Not since yours ceased to work, and mine ceased to be
something I could trust.
Red. Painting over the blues that once lived in these walls. I miss
those blues. The purity, the depth, the intensity of those blues. This
red is harsh. It is raw and unsettling.
Maybe one day, this red will soften, and a tinge of blue might shine through.
Maybe one day, the blue of your life and the red of your death might
merge together to create a purple I can almost bear to look at. Or maybe

blue will never look blue to me again. Maybe
accepting your death is
accepting that I am now colourblind, that my
brain sees red when there
is none. Every lake, every river, every perfectly
blue sky now tainted.
Maybe Red inhabits me now.
Maybe Blue is reserved for the living.

Foetal microchimerism

Your existence altered
the very cells in my body,
Why would your death
not irreversibly change me,
too?

Wildfire

I read an article
about wildfires,
that said
when a forest is
burned,
what comes back
may never resemble
what stood before.
What a perfect analogy
of us – your death
lit a fire in me
so strong,
that now
only
wasteland
remains.

Every version of me is yours

Signposts to older versions of myself are scattered
amongst the rubble remaining – the aftermath of the
tsunami that ripped through your existence.
One signpost labelled 'Hope'; the last time I felt your
heart beating and believed you might survive.
Surely, you would survive.
You have to survive.
'Normality' is the living room of the house we lived.
A soundtrack of laughter, nursery rhymes
and clapping reverberate around the empty space.
A quiet, contented love filling the room. This place is
safely - the time before, when this disease wasn't part
of us, when it didn't change who we were irrevocably.
Another signpost with the word 'rebirth' shows me the

hospital bed where you took your first breath in
this
world, and I took my first breath as a being
inexplicably
entwined with your own.

'Heartbreak' sends me to the day that your body
ceased
to exist in any form other than ash. A literal
piece of me
no longer takes the shape of my 8 month old
son, but
instead lies as the contents of a 12 x 12 cm white
box,
passed to me in a small white gift bag.
Because how else do you present a mother with
her son?
The last signpost I find is 'Forever' – and I am
uncontrollably
shaking, mid panic attack, heart thumping –
repeating the
same sentences over and over in my head;

"Your heart was beating 210 times per minute.
210 times in 60 seconds. 3 and a half beats
Every. Single. Second"

And yet here I am, wondering if my heart could
possibly

beat any faster.
Wondering if my arteries will rupture.
Wondering because that's now a possibility.
Wondering because if this could happen to you,
then why wouldn't it happen to me?
And wondering because why wasn't it me?
And wondering because it should have been me.
And wondering because it's been so long since I
held you and now only a 12 x 12 cm white box
gets
to hold you.

Wondering. Just wondering.

There are thousands of versions of who I used to
be, and not a single one makes sense without
you. How do I explain that I wish I had been
blind my
whole life so I didn't long for your smiling eyes;
that I
wish I had been deaf so I didn't know the joy
that a
single laugh could bring.
There are thousands of versions of who I used to
be.
Before this. Before the tidal wave tore through
our love.

A thousand versions of who I used to be.

And
yet,
every
version
of
me
is
yours.

Evolving grief

Those early days seem distant now; walks where my
legs could not carry the heaviness of our Truth -
grass
beneath my feet becoming a temporary place to rest my
head. Recently, I have leaned into this loss with a sense of
belonging. If I can't have you, then I will cradle this abyss
instead.

Mother tongue

If I could tear open my rib cage, I would
show them the wildflowers that
sprouted as a result of your existence.
The seeds that were sown through
the gentle need of your reaching
grasp, that bloomed further with every
smile-filled glance; a now extinct language
that only you spoke, and I translated.

What a loss for the 7.8 billion inhabitants
of this cruel world who never got to hear the
sweet lessons your language would teach them.
I listen for your mother tongue all around
me; it is nowhere to be found – and it pains
me more every day that it is fading from my
memory too quickly.

Time

August 6th 2019

It's 11AM on a Tuesday, and in twenty-nine minutes I will hold you for what I cannot believe will be the first time after carrying you so close for two hundred and seventy-six days. In between Entonox gasps and screams that I cannot possibly push a baby human out of my body, there are moments of unfiltered happiness; like when you father told me he doesn't know how I am doing this, how I am looking so beautiful, and for a second the world stopped spinning and there is no doubt that he is the best person I could ever have dreamt of finding to share this life – to share you – with.

It's 11am on a Tuesday, and I'm staring at the clock because watching the seconds pass is a good way to focus on something other than the pain, but also because I want to be able to pinpoint the exact moment my life became purposeful.

14th April 2020

It's 11AM on a Tuesday. I know it's 11AM because the room has a fading cleanliness to it, unlike at 10AM when the smell of disinfectant

overpowers us, or at 9am when the sound of
rustling plastic aprons, pens dancing across once
empty pieces of paper, and the abrupt coldness
of a piece of metal being pressed to your chest
disturbs our already broken slumber. It's 11AM
on a Tuesday, and for that one hour between
feeling like I'm tainting the sterile floors that
have just been mopped, and lunch – it feels still
and tranquil and calm.

It's just you and me, and this hospital room
we've been calling ours for weeks now. I say
ours, but its yours. I am just wherever you are.
It's just you and me, and a longing for our home
which in only a few short months will no longer
resemble our home – and will merely be the
house where you no longer live… Like every
house.

It's just you and me, and a pushchair that carries
the load when the literal heaviness of dread has
started to overtake my body. That pram will
travel one hundred and twenty miles with us, to
be abandoned at the end of a hospital bed that
you have since vacated – because how unfair it
would be to walk the winding corridors to the
awaiting two hour car journey with an empty
pushchair that will never again temporarily take
the weight of you from my arms.

It's just you and me. And even though we're
here, in this place so removed from normality,
this is the last time my world made sense.
27th July 2021
It's 11AM on a Tuesday, and my bones are
aching and my mind is racing, and the memory
of how it feels to have your hair brush my skin
as I breathe you in is getting further from my
reach. I am terrified of forgetting, and I am
terrified of remembering, and I wake in a panic
because I haven't fed for you for a really long
time. How irrational, when I know you are gone
– I feel the presence of your absence in every
beat of my heart.
It's 11AM on a Tuesday – and time has ceased to
exist as it once did; days merge into weeks, into
months, into years – and all that exists now is
the knowledge that you do not.

Kaleidoscope

Smiling eyes wide with wonder, your glow
reached
cavities that had never before seen the light of
day.
You were the magic I doubted ever existed; my
glittering kaleidoscope of beauty; a reflection of
the
man that I love.

Between sleeping and waking

It is always with me; the crushing reality that
you are no longer are.
I thought I would have just one second between
sleeping and
waking, where I would be blissfully unaware of
your death. I
thought, if that happened, perhaps I could live
for those seconds.
But those moments never came – as if every part
of my being,
on every level of consciousness, knows that you
are missing from
me.

The unanswerable questions of a bereaved parent

I am still his mother, I hear
them say. And I am, I guess.
But how do I parent a child
who is everywhere and nowhere?
How do I bridge the space
between this realm and theirs?
How do I feel his presence
and absence in equal measure?

Senseless

Everything is sharp these days – but I rarely feel
it's points. I see the
piercing blades of grief tear through my
figurative flesh and watch with
an inability to truly connect to the pain. I
acknowledge it's existence
(it's hard to ignore these knives as I place too
much pressure on the
wounds they are plugging) but am indifferent to
the lighting-white pain
that spreads to every nerve ending in my body.
This pain would have
disabled me at any of other point in my life, it
would have sent me into
a state of sheer panic because surely no one alive
has possibly
survived this level of torture. Yet here I am,
surviving. Occasionally, even
functioning.
Sometimes, there's a calm. A stillness that takes
over me when my mind
replays the way his eyes would give him away
before his lips had time to
form a smile. The way he would shuffle his body
closer to mine whilst he

was fast asleep – an instinct to be close to his
mother, the safest place he
knew.
And with that, I feel the blades – thousands of
them – raining down on me.
The pain is unbearable, and I sit with the agony,
and I breathe through the
pain whilst I whisper that I love him, because I
know that any moment now,
my brain will flip that switch to disconnect again
– but for this moment, it's
good to feel how much I miss him.
It's good to feel how much I miss him.
It's good to feel how much I love him.

Then it's gone, and I am merely a bystander
again – watching the torrent of
knives and I cannot stop them from slicing
through every part of my body. I
am unsure if anything can truly hurt me now –
you were my weakness, my
answer, my love. And now you are gone, there is
no part of me that can make
sense of something that is utterly senseless.
Everything is sharp.
And everything is dull.

A love letter to grief

I misunderstood you;
I saw you as an obstacle,
a never-ending mountain
to climb – a feat that could
never be achieved.

Still, you remained;
unwavering yet fluid,
shape-shifting your way,
daily, through the maze
of my nightmare.
But now, I can see you;
your invisible shape, the
exact outline of the
unending love I will carry
for him, always.

Permanency

What strikes me hardest is the permanency of
death.
I don't mean that I do not understand that he has
gone.
I know that his heart stopped beating. I know
that dying
isn't reversible. There's no pause button to stop
the world
from turning, time from passing, or the sun from
rising -
even though it makes no sense to me that these
things
could possibly continue without him. Instead, I
mean the
foreverness of my loss of him. The
overwhelming realisation
that this is

Never. Going. Away.

That there is nothing I will ever whole-heartedly
believe
in again, no cause that will ever matter in the
same way.

I lost more than you, more than our future, our dreams,
our should-have-could-have-would-have-beens.

My loss of you lost me myself, too.

Atomic #74

24

Sometimes, I carry our story around with grace.
The memory
of you only grazes at my skin – a jolt, a pinprick
– before love
overpowers it. Other times, it disables me. Like
every cell in my
body has been overtaken with Tungsten – and it
is an impossibility
to take another step through a realm that you no
longer exist in.

"You are so strong"

Let me just stop you there – because whilst I
realise that
your well-intentioned statement comes from a
good place,
reassuring me how 'well' I am doing – I can
assure you that
there is not even an ounce of my strength
involved in the
trauma of his story.
This was not a choice. This is something forced
upon me.
There was no strength when I cried silently at
the prospect
of losing him, trying desperately to control my
body's urge
to shake or heave because he had finally fallen
asleep on
my chest and if I moved even one centimetre, he
would
wake in pain.
There was no strength when tears streamed
down my face
because I had to hold him still whilst they
pierced his skin with

needles and he just cannot fathom why his sole protector is

letting – enabling – these people to hurt him.
There was no strength when I couldn't get him to stop crying;
He needs to stop crying. His heart can't take this level of stress.
Let's walk around. I'll sing to him whilst we walk. I'll calm him down.
Let's walk around. This cry doesn't sound right. I'll sing to him whilst
we walk. The door opens and I am screaming…
"HELP"
His heart can't take this level of stress. I'll calm him down. Let's
walk around. They need to me to put him down. I can't walk around.
I can't sing to him whilst we walk. There's no cry to not sound right
anymore. There are doctors flooding the room, obscuring my view
of him; our night-time playlist playing as the soundtrack of his death
beneath the composed but stern orders coming from the lead doctor.
And I am begging – begging – him to breathe. And I need to sit down,
because my legs have ceased to be something I am in control of, like

whether his heart will continue to beat. And I am
drinking water to
appease the nurse who is hugging me so tightly.
She knows what's going
to happen. And I am begging him to breathe, and
they keep stopping to
check his heart rate, and a second feels like an
hour waiting for the shout
that they had a response.
But they didn't.
And they continued.
And I am begging
– begging –
him to breathe.
She knows what's going to happen.
And then they stop.
Water – Begging – Nothing – Nothing –
Nothing.
Just him in my arms. His blood leaking into his
chest cavity after
forcing its way through the weakened arteries of
his heart that I
could not physically fix for him. What I would
have given would
have taken strength. What I would have endured,
you could call
strength. But sitting helplessly – hopelessly –
knowing all I can

give him is love and that that love will never be enough?
No.
There is no strength here.

Mine

You are every star,
You are every grain of sand,
You are every blade of grass.
You are every leaf falling from every tree,
You are every song that every bird will ever
sing.
You are the movement in the wind,
And the warmth of the sun.

You are mine, and you always will be.

Dust

I used to find magic in poetry;

Strings of letters forming words,
Forging a story that not even I knew the end of.

But no such story exists now.
The conclusion is always the same.

The ink has dried, pages empty.
The open-eyed wonder at the world…

disintegrated
– like you –
to dust.

My heart will keep beating

As sure as I can be
That the moon will keep rising,
And the birds will keep singing,
And the flowers will keep growing,
And my heart will keep beating,
I will miss you.

As sure as I can be
That the seasons will keep changing,
And the sun will keep burning,
And the time will keep passing,
And my heart will keep beating,
I will need you.

As sure as I can be
That the earth will keep spinning,
And the tides will keep pulling,
And the stars will keep shining,
And my heart will keep beating,
(Even when yours stopped)
I will love you.

My wishes for you, reader, through loss

Don't let them tell you that you are doing this
wrong,
or that everything happens for a reason. You do
not need
to look at the positive things in your life. This is
not a lesson
you needed to learn. Welcome in the crippling
pain, let it
make itself at home – it hurts because they
belonged here,
with you. Sit with it, when you can. And when
you can't, give
yourself grace. Know that your laughter does not
make you
'over' this. Joy and despair – gratitude and
misery – life and
death co-exist.

Forever altered

33

Darling boy,
I will never be the same,
and nor would I want to be.